STOIC WISDOM

STOIC WISDOM

Courage • Temperance • Justice • Wisdom

ABBIE HEADON

amber
BOOKS

Amber Books Ltd
United House
North Road
London N7 9DP
United Kingdom
www.amberbooks.co.uk
Facebook: amberbooks
YouTube: amberbooksltd
Instagram: amberbooksltd
X(Twitter): @amberbooks

MIX
Paper | Supporting responsible forestry
FSC® C017606
FSC
www.fsc.org

ISBN: 978-1-83886-718-8

Design & Editorial: Amber Books Ltd

Printed in China

TRADITIONAL CHINESE BOOKBINDING
This book has been produced using traditional Chinese bookbinding techniques, using a method that was developed during the Ming Dynasty (1368–1644) and remained in use until the adoption of Western binding techniques in the early 1900s. In traditional Chinese binding, single sheets of paper are printed on one side only, and each sheet is folded in half, with the printed pages on the outside. The book block is then sandwiched between two boards and sewn together through punched holes close to the cut edges of the folded sheets.

Contents

Introduction

When we call someone a 'stoic' with a small s, we tend to think first and foremost of their powers of endurance; a stoical person never complains, even in the toughest of circumstances. However, Stoic philosophy with a capital S has far more to it than simply putting up with difficult situations.

The founder of Stoicism was Zeno of Citium (c. 334–c. 262 BCE), who taught in an Athens marketplace with an open colonnade, known as the Stoa Poikile or Painted Porch, and the public philosophers of the Stoa became known as the Stoics.

Zeno and his successors Cleanthes (c. 330–c. 230 BCE) and Chrysippus (c. 279–c. 206 BCE) took inspiration from their Greek forebears Socrates and Plato and from the Cynics, and they described themselves as following in the Socratic tradition. Later, Stoicism would also flourish in Rome, particularly in the works of Seneca the Younger (c. 4 BCE–65 CE), Epictetus (c. 50–c. 135 CE) and Roman emperor Marcus Aurelius (121–180 CE), whose *Meditations* continue to be widely read today.

At the heart of Stoic philosophy is a belief that the universe is governed by reason, and defined by three key ideals: logic, ethics and physics. In Zeno's words, as described by Cicero, 'That which reasons is superior to that which does not; nothing is superior to the world; the world, therefore, reasons.' For Stoics, logical thought is a tool to help people achieve a life that is worth living, and an ethical approach ensures that that life will be a virtuous one. Finally, an understanding of physics is needed to appreciate what Stoics perceived to be the 'passive' and 'active' aspects of the universe, with the physical substance of creation being seen as passive and the primordial fire or 'world soul' being active.

This fundamental idea of using our faculty of reasoning to understand and come to terms with the world we live in is perhaps what has given Stoicism such a lasting legacy and enduring popularity. Today, for many of us, it can feel as if the events of our personal and professional lives, not to mention the wider world as a whole, are evolving faster and faster, in directions we can neither control nor predict. Stoicism teaches that although the events that we will encounter during our lives are outside our control, we have one key domain where each of us is unassailable: in our choice of how to respond to the things that happen to us. In the words of Epictetus, 'It is not the things themselves that disturb men, but their judgements about these things.'

Followers of Stoic philosophy aim to be guided by the four cardinal virtues of courage, temperance, justice and wisdom, and to free themselves from the passions of distress, fear, lust and delight. With its focus on clear thinking and positive action, it's easy to see why Stoicism is popular today as a way of dealing with the complexity of the world. It may not always be possible to govern our emotional responses to life's ups and downs, because we're human, after all, but Stoic philosophy can offer some tools to help us regroup, take a deep breath, and find a way forward in challenging times.

'Zeno was the first ... to designate as the end "life in agreement with nature" (or living agreeably to nature), which is the same as a virtuous life, virtue being the goal towards which nature guides us. So too Cleanthes in his treatise *On Pleasure*, as also Posidonius, and Hecato in his work *On Ends*.'

– Diogenes Laërtius, 'Lives of the Eminent Philosophers', 7.87

'Philosophy neither rejects nor selects anyone; its light shines for all. Socrates was no aristocrat. Cleanthes worked at a well and served as a hired man watering a garden.'

– Seneca, 'Moral Letters to Lucilius', 44.2–3

'He consulted the oracle to know what he should do to attain the best life, and that the god's response was that he should take on the complexion of the dead.'

– Diogenes Laërtius describing Zeno of Citium in 'Lives of the Eminent Philosophers', 7.2

'He is free who lives as he wills, who is subject neither to compulsion, nor hindrance, nor force, whose choices are unhampered, whose desires attain their end, whose aversions do not fall into what they would avoid.'

– *Epictetus, 'The Discourses', 4.1.1*

'Chrysippus and Diogenes were the earliest and firmest advocates of the contempt of glory; and maintained that, amongst all pleasures, there was none more dangerous nor more to be avoided than that which proceeds from the approbation of others.'

– Michel de Montaigne, 'Essays', Book 2, Chapter 16

'Just when the gods had ceased to be, and the Christ had not yet come, there was a unique moment in history, between Cicero and Marcus Aurelius, when man stood alone. Nowhere else do I find that particular grandeur.'

– *Gustave Flaubert, letter to Madame Roger des Genettes*

'What was best in the Cynic doctrine passed over into Stoicism, which was an altogether more complete and rounded philosophy.'

– Bertrand Russell,
'A History of Western Philosophy', Book 1, Part 3

'If any man could arrive at the exterior limit, or take the wings of a bird and fly upward, like a fish who puts his head out and sees the world, he would see a world beyond; and, if the nature of man could sustain this sight, he would acknowledge that this was the place of the true heaven and the true light and the true stars.'

– Plato quoting Socrates in 'Phaedo'

'"That which reasons is superior to that which does not; nothing is superior to the world; the world, therefore, reasons." By the same rule the world may be proved to be wise, happy, and eternal; for the possession of all these qualities is superior to the want of them; and nothing is superior to the world; the inevitable consequence of which argument is, that the world, therefore, is a Deity.'

– Cicero quoting and commenting on Zeno of Citium in 'On the Nature of the Gods', 2.8

'Lead me, Zeus, and you too, Destiny,
To wherever your decrees have assigned me.
I follow readily, but if I choose not,
Wretched though I am, I must follow still.
Fate guides the willing, but drags the unwilling.'

– Cleanthes, 'Hymn to Zeus'

'For he says that the divine power is placed in reason, and in the spirit and mind of universal nature; that the world, with a universal effusion of its spirit, is God; that the superior part of that spirit, which is the mind and reason, is the great principle of nature, containing and preserving the chain of all things; that the divinity is the power of fate, and the necessity of future events.'

– Cicero quoting Chrysippus of Soli
in 'On the Nature of the Gods', 1.15

'Just as a mark is not set up in order to be missed, so neither does the nature of evil arise in the universe.'

– *Epictetus, 'The Encheiridion, or Manual', 27*

'The work of the gods is full of Providence: the work of Fortune is not divorced from Nature or the spinning and winding of the threads ordained by Providence. All flows from that other world; and there is, besides, necessity and the wellbeing of the whole universe, whereof you are a part.'

– Marcus Aurelius, 'Meditations', 2.3

'All things that exist will very swiftly change; either they will pass into vapour, if we presume that matter is a whole, or else they will be dispersed into their atoms.'

– Marcus Aurelius, 'Meditations', 6.4

'They hold that there are two principles in the universe, the active principle and the passive. The passive principle, then, is a substance without quality, i.e. matter, whereas the active is the reason inherent in this substance, that is God. For he is everlasting and is the artificer of each several thing throughout the whole extent of matter.'

– Diogenes Laërtius on the Stoics
in 'Lives of the Eminent Philosophers', 7.134

'The sun is pure fire: so Posidonius in the seventh book of his Celestial Phenomena. And it is larger than the earth ... Moreover it is spherical in shape like the world itself according to this same author and his school. That it is fire is proved by its producing all the effects of fire; that it is larger than the earth by the fact that all the earth is illuminated by it; nay more, the heaven beside.'

– *Diogenes Laërtius, 'Lives of the Eminent Philosophers', 7.144*

'Full across the way of Virtue the immortal gods
have set the sweat of the brow; long and steep is the path
that reaches to her, and rough at the beginning;
but when you reach the highest point, hard though it is,
in the end it becomes easy.'

– *Hesiod, 'Works and Days', 289–292*

'Living virtuously is equivalent to living in accordance with experience of the actual course of nature, as Chrysippus says in the first book of his *De finibus*; for our individual natures are parts of the nature of the whole universe.'

– *Diogenes Laërtius, 'Lives of the Eminent Philosophers'*, 7.87

'Riches are a cause of evil, not because, of themselves, they do any evil, but because they goad men on so that they are ready to do evil. For the efficient cause, which necessarily produces harm at once, is one thing, and the antecedent cause is another.'

– Seneca quoting Posidonius in 'Moral Letters to Lucilius', 87.31

'The definition of a perturbation, as Zeno, I think, has rightly determined it, is thus: That a perturbation is a commotion of the mind against nature, in opposition to right reason; or, more briefly, thus, that a perturbation is a somewhat too vehement appetite; and when he says somewhat too vehement, he means such as is at a greater distance from the constant course of nature.'

– Cicero, 'Tusculan Disputations', Book 4.21

'But nothing is more perfect than the world, and nothing better than virtue. Virtue, therefore, is an attribute of the world. But human nature is not perfect, and nevertheless virtue is produced in it: with how much greater reason, then, do we conceive it to be inherent in the world!'

– Cicero, 'On the Nature of the Gods', 2.14.

'Of all existing things some are good, some evil, and some indifferent. Now the good things are virtues and what partakes of them, the evil are vice and what partakes of vice, and the indifferent lie between these: wealth, health, life, death, pleasure, pain.'

– Aulus Gellius quoting Epictetus, 'Attic Nights', 1.2.9

'Bear in mind, that if through toil you accomplish a good deed, that toil will quickly pass from you, the good deed will not leave you so long as you live; but if through pleasure you do anything dishonourable, the pleasure will quickly pass away, that dishonourable act will remain with you for ever.'

– *Aulus Gellius quoting Cato the Younger, 'Attic Nights', 16.1.4*

'What then is peculiar to man? Reason. When this is right and has reached perfection, man's felicity is complete. … This perfect reason is called virtue, and is likewise that which is honourable.'

– Seneca, 'Moral Letters to Lucilius', 76.10

'Do not seek to have everything that happens happen as you wish, but wish for everything to happen as it actually does happen, and your life will be serene.'

– Epictetus, 'The Encheiridion, or Manual', 8

'Virtue, in the first place, is in one sense the perfection of anything in general, say of a statue; again, it may be non-intellectual, like health, or intellectual, like prudence.'

– Diogenes Laërtius, 'Lives of the Eminent Philosophers', 7.90

'...The easy, smooth, and descending way by which the regular steps of a sweet disposition of nature are conducted is not that of a true virtue; she requires a rough and stormy passage.'

– Michel de Montaigne, 'Essays', Book 2, Chapter 11

'... The easiest way for us to gain happiness is to learn how to want the things we already have.'

– William B. Irvine

'The dearest thing to every animal is its own constitution and its consciousness thereof.'

– Chrysippus, quoted in Diogenes Laërtius, 'Lives of the Eminent Philosophers', 7.85

'By Fate I mean … a certain order and series of causes – for cause linked to cause produces all things: and in this connexion of cause consists the constant truth which flows through all eternity. From whence it follows that nothing happens which is not predestined to happen; and in the same way nothing is predestined to happen, the nature of which does not contain the efficient causes of its happening.'

– Cicero, 'On Divination', Book 1.55

'The mind employs the senses, and also creates the sciences as a second set of senses, and strengthens the structurc of philosophy itself to the point where it may produce virtue, the sole source of the ordering of the whole of life.'

– Cicero, 'Academica', 2.31

'I have placed every good thing within your own breasts: it is your good fortune not to need any good fortune.'

– Seneca, 'Of Providence', 6

‘Is my understanding sufficient for this or not? If it is sufficient, I employ it for the task as an instrument bestowed on me by Universal Nature. But if it is insufficient, either I withdraw from the task in favour of one who can accomplish it better … or else I do it as best I can, taking to help me one who by using my intelligence to assist him can do what is now opportune and beneficial for the general public.’

– Marcus Aurelius, ‘Meditations’, 7.5

'He who does not know that the Universe exists, does not know where he is. He who does not know the purpose of the Universe, does not know who he is nor what the Universe is. He who fails in any one of these respects could not even declare the purpose of his own birth.'

– *Marcus Aurelius, 'Meditations', 8.52*

'Philosophy, they say, is like an animal, Logic corresponding to the bones and sinews, Ethics to the fleshy parts, Physics to the soul. Another simile they use is that of an egg: the shell is Logic, next comes the white, Ethics, and the yolk in the centre is Physics. Or, again, they liken Philosophy to a fertile field: Logic being the encircling fence, Ethics the crop, Physics the soil or the trees.'

– Diogenes Laërtius, 'Lives of the Eminent Philosophers', 7.40

'All other knowledge is hurtful to him who has not the science of goodness.'

– Michel de Montaigne, 'Essays', Book 1, Chapter 24

'Zeno … used to illustrate to his disciples the steps to knowledge by means of gestures. Displaying his right hand with the fingers outstretched he would say, "That is a phantasy," then contracting the fingers a little, "That is assent," then having closed the fist, "That is comprehension," then clasping the fist closely with the left hand, he would add, "That is knowledge."'

– St George Stock, 'A Guide to Stoicism'

'Examine the definitions of courage: you will find it does not require the assistance of passion. Courage is, then, an affection of mind that endures all things, being itself in proper subjection to the highest of all laws.'

– Cicero quoting Sphaerus in 'Tusculan Disputations', Book 4.24

'Live with Chrysippus, with Posidonius: they will make you acquainted with things earthly and things heavenly; they will bid you work hard over something more than neat turns of language and phrases mouthed forth for the entertainment of listeners; they will bid you be stout of heart and rise superior to threats.'

– Seneca, 'Moral Letters to Lucilius', 104.22

'Just as so many rivers, so many showers of rain from the clouds, such a number of medicinal springs, do not alter the taste of the sea, indeed, do not so much as soften it, so the pressure of adversity does not affect the mind of a brave man; for the mind of a brave man maintains its balance and throws its own complexion over all that takes place, because it is more powerful than any external circumstances.'

– Seneca, 'Of Providence', 2

'I must die: must I, then, die groaning too? I must be fettered: and wailing too? I must go into exile: does anyone, then, keep me from going with a smile and cheerful and serene? "Tell your secrets." I say not a word; for this is under my control. "But I will fetter you." What is that you say, man? Fetter me? My leg you will fetter, but my moral purpose not even Zeus himself has power to overcome.'

– *Epictetus, 'The Discourses', 1.1.21–23*

'Be like the headland on which the waves continually break, but it stands firm and about it the boiling waters sink to sleep.'

– Marcus Aurelius, 'Meditations', 4.49

'The reason why they characterise the perfect good as beautiful is that it has in full all the "factors" required by nature or has perfect proportion. Of the beautiful there are (say they) four species, namely, what is just, courageous, orderly and wise; for it is under these forms that fair deeds are accomplished.'

– *Diogenes Laërtius, 'Lives of the Eminent Philosophers', 7.100*

'Yes, as my swift days near their goal,
'Tis all that I implore;
In life and death a chainless soul,
With courage to endure.'

– Emily Brontë, 'The Old Stoic'

‘When we are no longer able to change a situation – we are challenged to change ourselves.’

– *Viktor Frankl*

'The being of all virtues, and chiefly of temperance, depends on the practice of them.'

– Xenophon quoting Socrates in 'Memorabilia', 1.3.10

'The things that are indispensable require no elaborate pains for their acquisition; it is only the luxuries that call for labour. Follow nature, and you will need no skilled craftsmen.'

– Seneca, 'Moral Letters to Lucilius', 90.16

'No one entrusts a secret to a drunken man; but one will entrust a secret to a good man; therefore, the good man will not get drunk.'

– Seneca quoting Zeno of Citium, 'Moral Letters to Lucilius', 83.9

'Wealth is able to buy the pleasures of eating, drinking and other sensual pursuits – yet can never afford a cheerful spirit or freedom from sorrow.'

– *Gaius Musonius Rufus*

'Remember that you ought to behave in life as you would at a banquet. As something is being passed around it comes to you; stretch out your hand and take a portion of it politely. It passes on; do not detain it.'

– Epictetus, 'The Encheiridion, or Manual', 15

'I will begin to speak when I am not going to say what were better left unsaid.'

– Plutarch, quoting Cato the Younger in 'Life of Cato the Younger', 4

'Errors of appetite are graver than errors of temper. For clearly one who loses his temper is turning away from Reason with a kind of pain and inward spasm; whereas he who offends through appetite is the victim of pleasure and is clearly more vicious in a way and more effeminate in his wrong-doing.'

– Marcus Aurelius quoting Theophrastus in 'Meditations', 2.10

'There was a gourmand so greedy that he left nothing for his table companions. A large fish having been served, Zeno took it up as if he were about to eat the whole. When the other looked at him, "What do you suppose," said he, "those who live with you feel every day, if you cannot put up with my gourmandise in this single instance?"'

– Diogenes Laërtius, 'Lives of the Eminent Philosophers', 7.19

'The worst state of man is that wherein he loses the knowledge and government of himself.'

– Michel de Montaigne, 'Essays', Book 2, Chapter 2

'One should never do wrong in return, nor mistreat any man, no matter how one has been mistreated by him.'

– Plato quoting Socrates in 'Crito', 49c–d

'But the true Good is not found in trees or in dumb animals, for the Good which exists in them is called "good" only by courtesy. "Then what is it?" you say. Simply that which is in accord with the nature of each. The real Good cannot find a place in dumb animals – not by any means; its nature is more blest and is of a higher class. And where there is no place for reason, the Good does not exist.'

– Seneca, 'Moral Letters to Lucilius', 124.13

'The good man will do his duty without disturbance or fear, and he will perform the duty of a good man, so as to do nothing unworthy of a man. My father will be murdered: then I will defend him: he has been slain, then I will avenge him, not because I am grieved, but because it is my duty.'

– Seneca, 'Of Anger', 1.12

'Now just as it is the nature of every soul to assent to the true, dissent from the false, and to withhold judgement in a matter of uncertainty, so it is its nature to be moved with desire toward the good, with aversion toward the evil, and feel neutral toward what is neither evil nor good.'

– Epictetus, 'The Discourses', 3.3.2

'Endeavour to persuade them, but act even if they themselves are unwilling, when the rule of justice so directs.'

– Marcus Aurelius, 'Meditations', 6.50

'And so from [Universal Nature] is the birth of Justice, and from Justice the rest of the virtues have their existence; for Justice will not be preserved if we are concerned for indifferent objects or are easily deceived by them or are liable to stumble or to change.'

– Marcus Aurelius, 'Meditations', 11.10

‘The notions of justice and goodness come by nature.’

– Diogenes Laërtius, ‘Lives of the Eminent Philosophers’, 7.53

'It is a tenet of theirs that between virtue and vice there is nothing intermediate … For, say the Stoics, just as a stick must be either straight or crooked, so a man must be either just or unjust. Nor again are there degrees of justice and injustice; and the same rule applies to the other virtues.'

– *Diogenes Laërtius, 'Lives of the Eminent Philosophers', 7.127*

'Anyone who holds a true opinion without understanding is like a blind man on the right road.'

– Plato quoting Socrates in 'Republic', 506c

'The reason why we have two ears and only one mouth is that we may listen the more and talk the less.'

– *Diogenes Laërtius quoting Zeno of Citium in 'Lives of the Eminent Philosophers', 7.23*

'It is one of their maxims that the wise are friends to the wise, though unknown to each other; for as nothing is more amiable than virtue, he who possesses it is worthy our love, to whatever country he belongs.'

– *Cicero on the Stoics, 'On the Nature of the Gods', 1.44.*

'God has the same purpose as the wise man, that is, to prove that the things which the herd covets and dreads are neither good nor bad in themselves.'

– Seneca, 'Of Providence', 5

'It is not the things themselves that disturb men, but their judgements about these things.'

– Epictetus, 'The Encheiridion, or Manual', 5

'[A wise man] remembers that all reasonable beings are akin to himself, and that although to care for all men is in accord with man's nature, he is to cling not to the opinion of all men, but only of men who live in accord with Nature.'

– Marcus Aurelius, 'Meditations', 3.4

'Once for all I wish to be blind to many things. Wisdom sets bounds even to knowledge.'

– Friedrich Nietzsche, 'Maxims and Missiles', 5

'If you can talk with crowds and keep your virtue,
Or walk with Kings – nor lose the common touch,
If neither foes nor loving friends can hurt you,
If all men count with you, but none too much:
If you can fill the unforgiving minute
With sixty seconds' worth of distance run,
Yours is the Earth and everything that's in it,
And – which is more – you'll be a Man, my son!'

– from Rudyard Kipling, 'If—'

'No evil is glorious; but death is glorious; therefore death is no evil.'

– *Seneca quoting Zeno of Citium in 'Moral Letters to Lucilius', 82.9*

'If I knew that it was fated for me to be sick, I would even wish for it; for the foot also, if it had intelligence, would volunteer to get muddy.'

– *Chrysippus of Soli, quoted in Epictetus, 'Discourses', ii. 6. 10*

'The first thing which philosophy undertakes to give is fellow-feeling with all men; in other words, sympathy and sociability. We part company with our promise if we are unlike other men.'

– Seneca, 'Moral Letters to Lucilius', 5.4

'Keep before your eyes day by day death and exile, and everything that seems terrible, but most of all death; and then you will never have any abject thought, nor will you yearn for anything beyond measure.'

– Epictetus, 'The Encheiridion, or Manual', 21

'Whenever you are obliged by circumstances to be in a way troubled, quickly return to yourself, and do not, more than you are obliged, fall out of step; for you will be more master of the measure by continually returning to it.'

– Marcus Aurelius, 'Meditations', 6.11

'That which does not kill me, makes me stronger.'

– Friedrich Nietzsche, 'Maxims and Missiles', 8

'Through a long life I have thoroughly wrought my will,
From Nature's hand refusing all rich fruits,
As from my labours, or man's kindliness,
Receiving but the means for innocent food,
Thus following Crates' and great Zeno's course,

As rigidly as link doth follow link,
When seamen raise an anchor to the prow;
Or as the shadow of the hero's spear
Beneath its singing, flies to the same mark.'

– from Richard Henry Horne, 'The Last Words of Cleanthes'

‘A Stoic is someone who transforms fear into prudence, pain into transformation, mistakes into initiation, and desire into undertaking.’

– Nassim Nicholas Taleb

'He who has lived as a true philosopher has reason to be of good cheer when he is about to die, and that after death he may hope to receive the greatest good in the other world.'

– Plato quoting Socrates in 'Phaedo'

'Without philosophy the mind is sickly, and the body, too, though it may be very powerful, is strong only as that of a madman or a lunatic is strong. This, then, is the sort of health you should primarily cultivate; the other kind of health comes second, and will involve little effort, if you wish to be well physically.'

– Seneca, 'Moral Letters to Lucilius', 15.1–2

'Each day acquire something that will fortify you against poverty, against death, indeed against other misfortunes as well; and after you have run over many thoughts, select one to be thoroughly digested that day.'

– *Seneca, 'Moral Letters to Lucilius', 2.4*

'Only by exhibiting actions in harmony with the sound words which he has received will anyone be helped by philosophy.'

– *Gaius Musonius Rufus*

'On no occasion call yourself a philosopher, and do not, for the most part, talk among laymen about your philosophic principles, but do what follows from your principles.'

– *Epictetus, 'The Encheiridion, or Manual', 46*

'In the conviction that it is possible you may depart from life at once, act and speak and think in every case accordingly.'

– Marcus Aurelius, 'Meditations', 2.11

'Were I to live my life over again, I should live it just as I have lived it; I neither complain of the past, nor do I fear the future; and if I am not much deceived, I am the same within that I am without.'

– Michel de Montaigne, 'Essays', Book 3, Chapter 2

'Live as if you were living a second time, and as though you had acted wrongly the first time.'

– Viktor Frankl

'Don't let the noise of others' opinions drown out your own inner voice.'

– Steve Jobs, Stanford University commencement speech, 2005

'How should a person live? … the ancient traditions are some of the best answers that man has come up with.'

– Ryan Holiday

Picture Credits

Alamy: 5 (Giorgio G), 8 (FOST), 12 (Album), 13 (Universal Art Archive), 14 (Svintage Archive), 19 (The Picture Art Collection), 26 (pxl.store), 32 (Stefano Ravera), 35 (Alexander Staridas), 37 (David Gee), 39 (Plrang GFX), 40 (Penta Springs), 44 (Science History Images), 48 (Erin Babnik), 50 (S. Forster), 61 (piemags), 69 (Album), 72 (Mark Davidson), 75 (Cristiano Fronteddu), 77 (Lanmas), 84 (Science History Images), 86 (Giorgio G), 88 (Alex Ramsay), 89 (Noel Bennett)

Dreamstime: 23 (AnnaOm), 33 (Magryt), 47 (Cortespr), 53 (Rruntsch), 56 (Madrabothair), 70 (Kostas1gr), 82 (Wowinside)

Getty Images: 16 (Universal History Archive), 22 (Heritage Images), 30 (jopstock), 31 (PHAS), 54 (De Agostini), 58 (Michael Nicholson), 71 & 87 (De Agostini), 91 (Fine Art Images), 92 (De Agostini),

Metropolitan Museum of New York: 17, 20, 25, 28, 29, 36, 38, 43, 45, 51, 55, 63-68, 73, 76, 78-80, 83, 85, 90, 94, 95

Public Domain: 57, 59, 74

Rijksmuseum, Amsterdam: 34, 62

Shutterstock: 9 (Artmim), 10 (Nita Yuko), 11 (Brian A Jackson), 15 (Daniel Huebner), 18 (Rapit Design), 21 (Stas Tolstnev), 24 (Boule), 27 (TuiPanthida), 41 (Mltz), 42 (lukaszimilena), 46 (David Andres Gutierrez), 49 (Nadezhda Bolotina), 52 (Snehit Photos), 81 (CeltStudio), 93 (Ainsley Gritter)

Walters Art Museum, Baltimore: 60